ABRAHAM LINCOLN

PEOPLE WHO MADE A DIFFERENCE

David and Patricia Armentrout

Rourke Publishing LLC
Vero Beach, Florida 32964

PHOTO CREDITS:
©PhotoDisc, Inc.
©James P. Rowan
©Library of Congress

EDITORIAL SERVICES:
Pamela Schroeder

Library of Congress Cataloging-in-Publication Data

Armentrout David, 1962
   Abraham Lincoln / David & Patricia Armentrout
      p. cm. — (People who made a difference)
   Includes index
   ISBN 1-58952-051-3
   1. Lincoln, Abraham, 1809-1865 — Juvenile literature. 2. Presidents—United States—
Biography—Juvenile literature.[1. Lincoln, Abraham, 1809-1865. 2. Presidents.]
I. Armentrout,Patricia, 1960- II. Title.

E457.905.A75 2001
973.7'092—dc21   2001018583
[B]

Printed in the USA

TABLE OF CONTENTS

Who is Abraham Lincoln?   5

Young Abraham   6

Learning on His Own   9

Law and Politics   11

Lincoln Spoke Against Slavery   12

President Lincoln   14

Freed Slaves   17

Gettysburg Address   18

Lincoln's Death   20

Important Dates to Remember   22

Glossary   23

Index   24

Further Reading/Websites to Visit   24

WHO IS ABRAHAM LINCOLN?

Abraham Lincoln was the 16th president of the United States. He fought to end slavery in America. He served during the **Civil War** (1861-1865). He gave a speech known as the Gettysburg Address. Many people feel Abraham Lincoln was the country's greatest president.

This famous white marble statue of President Lincoln is in the center hall of the Lincoln Memorial in Washington, D.C.

YOUNG ABRAHAM

Abraham Lincoln was born February 12, 1809. His parents were farmers. They lived in a one-room cabin in the Kentucky backwoods.

As young children Abraham and his older sister Sarah helped farm the fields. They spent little time going to school.

When Abraham was seven the family moved to Indiana. Abraham helped his father build a new home. He chopped down trees and split logs.

Lincoln's boyhood home in Knob Creek, Kentucky.

LEARNING ON HIS OWN

Abraham didn't go to school often, but he read all the time. He read about many things, including George Washington.

In 1818 Abraham's mother died. A year later his father married Sarah Bush Johnston. She had three children of her own. Sarah was very good to Abraham. She told him to keep reading.

LAW AND POLITICS

The Lincoln family moved to Illinois in 1830. After a year Abraham left home. Lincoln was a lawyer in Springfield. He met Mary Todd in Springfield. They were married in 1842. Abraham and Mary had 4 sons by 1853.

Lincoln loved **politics**. He served on the Illinois **legislature**. He was a congressman and ran for senator.

Mary Todd and Abraham Lincoln were married in 1842.

LINCOLN SPOKE AGAINST SLAVERY

The United States outlawed bringing new slaves into the country in the early 1800s. However, slavery was still in some states. Southern **plantation** owners had slaves. They did not want to see slavery end. Most northerners were against slavery, including Lincoln.

Lincoln spoke out against slavery. Lincoln wanted new states to join the Union as free states and not slave states.

Abraham Lincoln was known for his honesty and was often called "Honest Abe".

PRESIDENT LINCOLN

Lincoln ran for president in 1860 and won. He became president on March 4, 1861.

President Lincoln fought to keep the country together. However, eleven southern states left the Union. They formed the Confederate States of America. Both sides built armies, and the Civil War began April 12, 1861.

President Lincoln is shown here with his son Thomas.

FREED SLAVES

Slavery had split the country in two. President Lincoln could end slavery right away. However, he knew he would lose the support of some states. Lincoln thought that the southern states would leave the Union forever if he ended slavery.

President Lincoln finally created the **Emancipation Proclamation**. This proclamation said that the slaves of the Confederate states were free.

The Emancipation Proclamation was the beginning of the end of slavery in the U.S.

GETTYSBURG ADDRESS

The bloodiest battle of the Civil War was fought at Gettysburg, Pennsylvania. When it was over, thousands of soldiers lay dead on the battlefield.

Four months later people went to Gettysburg to honor the dead. President Lincoln spoke for only two minutes. However, his speech, called the Gettysburg Address, is now a special event in American history.

A painting of the battle at Gettysburg.

LINCOLN'S DEATH

On April 14th the President and Mrs. Lincoln went to a play. John Wilkes Booth, an actor who supported the south, shot Lincoln that night. President Lincoln died April 15, 1865.

Lincoln supported an **amendment** to stop slavery across the nation. After his death, on December 8, 1865, the Thirteenth Amendment to the **Constitution** became law.

This drawing shows John Wilkes Booth shooting President Lincoln.

Maj. Rathbone.   Miss Harris.   Mrs Lincoln   President.   Assassin.

THE ASSASSINATION OF PRESIDENT LINCOLN,

AT FORD'S THEATRE WASHINGTON. D.C. APRIL 14TH 1865.

Entered according to Act of Congress AD 1865 by Currier & Ives in the Clerks Office of the District Court of the United States for the Southern District of N.Y.

Published by Currier & Ives. 152 Nassau St New York

IMPORTANT DATES TO REMEMBER

1809	Born in Kentucky (February 12)
1816	Moved to Indiana
1830	Moved to Illinois
1842	Married Mary Todd
1861	Became president (March 4)
1861	Civil War began (April 12)
1863	Issued the Emancipation Proclamation (January 1)
1863	Gave the Gettysburg Address speech (November 19)
1865	The Civil War ended (April 9)
1865	Died in Washington, D.C. (April 15)
1865	Thirteenth Amendment became law

GLOSSARY

amendment (eh MEND ment) — a change or correction to a law

Constitution (KAHN steh TOO shen) — a list of laws

Civil War (SIV el WOR) — a war between the United States of America (Union) and eleven southern states (Confederacy)

Emancipation Proclamation (i MAN seh PAY shen PRAHK leh MAY shen) — a document issued by President Lincoln that freed, or emancipated, slaves

legislature (LEJ is LAY cher) — part of the government that makes laws and brings them into action

plantation (plan TAY shen) — a large farm that is worked by people living on it

politics (PAHL eh TIKS) — making and guiding government plans and laws

INDEX

Booth, John Wilkes   20

Civil War   5, 14, 18

Confederate States   14, 17

Emancipation Proclamation   17

Gettysburg Address   5, 18

Lincoln, Mary Todd   11

slavery   5, 12, 17, 20

Thirteenth Amendment   20

Further Reading

Bennett, Russell. *Abraham Lincoln.* Gareth Stevens, Milwaukee ©1992

Lee, Susan. *Abraham Lincoln.* Childrens Press, Chicago ©1978

Freedman, Russell. *Lincoln, A Photobiography*. Clarion Books, NY ©1987

Websites To Visit

•http://members.aol.com/RVSNorton/Lincoln2.html

•http://lincoln.lib.niu.edu/

About The Authors

David and Patricia Armentrout specialize in nonfiction writing. They have had several books published for primary school reading. They reside in Cincinnati, Ohio with their two children.